TUNIIT

WRITTEN BY
Rebecca Hainnu

ILLUSTRATED BY
Germaine Arnaktauyok

Published by Inhabit Education | www.inhabiteducation.com

Inhabit Education (Iqaluit), P.O. Box 2129, Iqaluit, Nunavut, X0A 1H0
(Toronto), 191 Eglinton Avenue East, Suite 301, Toronto, Ontario, M4P 1K1

Design and layout copyright © 2017 Inhabit Education
Text copyright © Inhabit Education
Illustrations by Germaine Arnaktauyok © Inhabit Education

Printed in Canada.

ISBN: 978-1-77266-551-2

INHABIT
EDUCATION

Long ago, a group of people called Tuniit lived in Nunavut. It was their home for hundreds of years before Inuit arrived. But there are no Tuniit in Nunavut today. Who were they? What were they like? Where did they go?

2

We don't know why Tuniit disappeared.
But we can learn about them through
stories elders tell about long ago.
We can also look at the things Tuniit
left behind to see how they lived.

Did You Know?

Stories that are told and passed down from one generation to the next are called oral history.

Did You Know?

When we are talking about one person, we use the word "Tuniq."

Inuit say Tuniit were excellent hunters. Tuniit hunted caribou, muskox, polar bear, walrus, and whale.

Some stories say Tuniit were much bigger than Inuit. Some stories say Tuniit were smaller than Inuit. Some stories even say Tuniit could change their size! But all stories agree on one thing. Tuniit were very, very strong.

Inuit stories say that a Tuniq man could carry a whole walrus all by himself! One story even tells of a Tuniq hunter who caught a polar bear without any weapons. He carried the bear home on his shoulders.

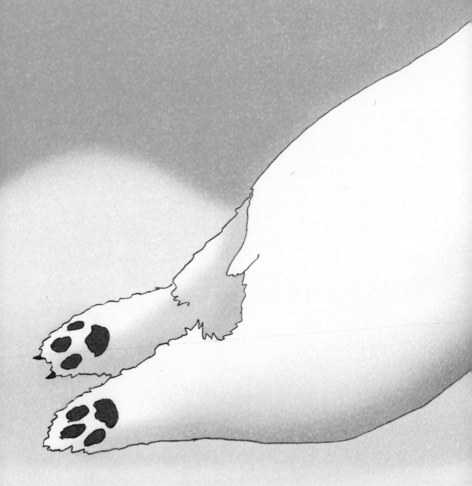

Did You Know?

Stories tell about Tuniit sleeping with their feet in the air to help them stay fast!

Tuniit were also very fast. They didn't need bows and arrows or sled dogs because they could catch up to animals just by running. They could even catch a fleeing caribou.

Stories say that Tuniit were shy around Inuit. Tuniit lived in different camps from Inuit. Tuniit didn't marry Inuit. Tuniit even spoke a different language from Inuit.

Did You Know?

Another name for Tuniit is Sivullirmiut. That means "people who came before us" in the Inuit language.

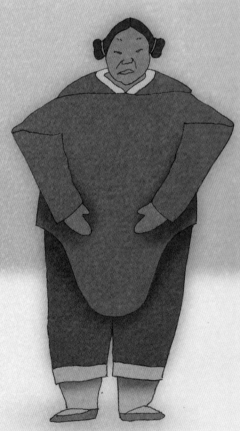

The remains of Tuniit camps still exist in Nunavut. Tuniit made houses for the winter. The houses were partly underground. The walls were made out of heavy boulders. Several families would live together in the same house.

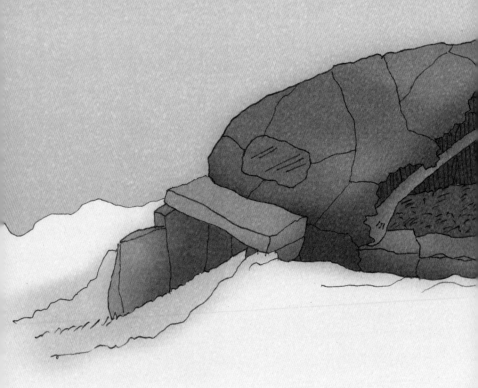

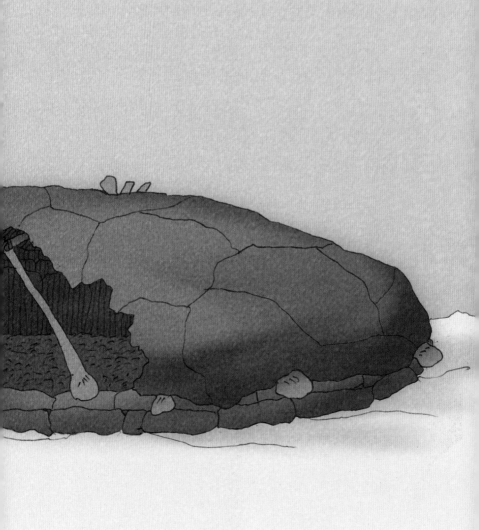

In summer, Tuniit lived in tents.
They would move their camps as they
followed the animals they hunted.

This way, they were always close to the animals. Tuniit set their tents up in rings, just like Inuit tents.

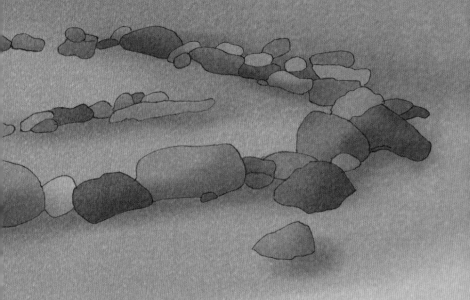

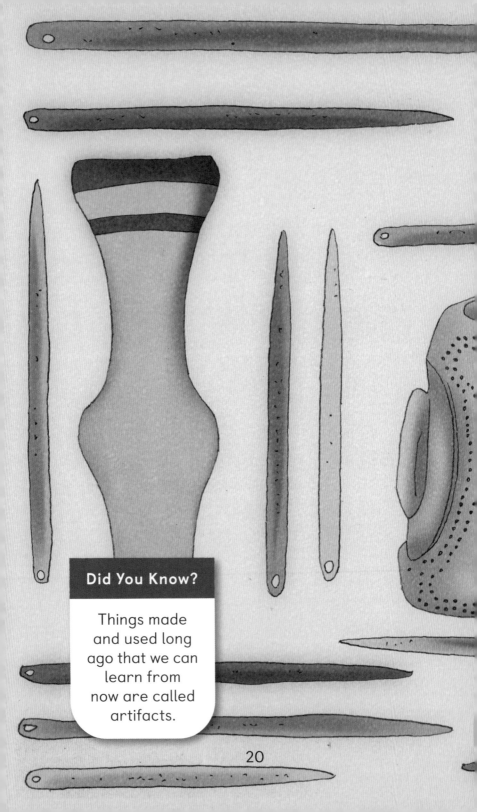

Did You Know?

Things made and used long ago that we can learn from now are called artifacts.

Tuniit used sewing needles that they made from bone. They used hunting knives that they made from slate or ivory.

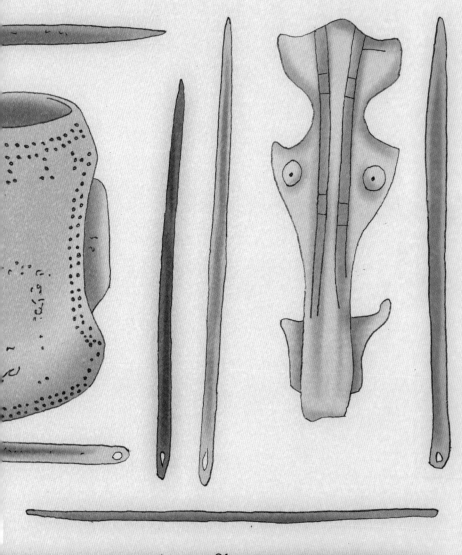

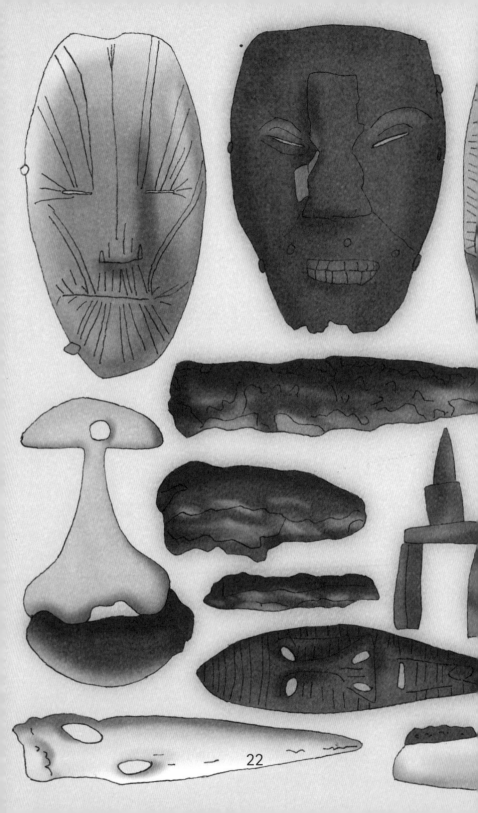

22

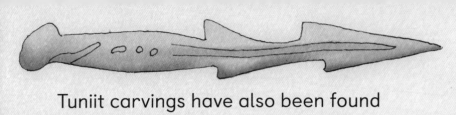

Tuniit carvings have also been found throughout Nunavut. Tuniit made figurines shaped like people and animals. They also carved faces into their tool handles. They even carved faces onto boulders and cliffs.

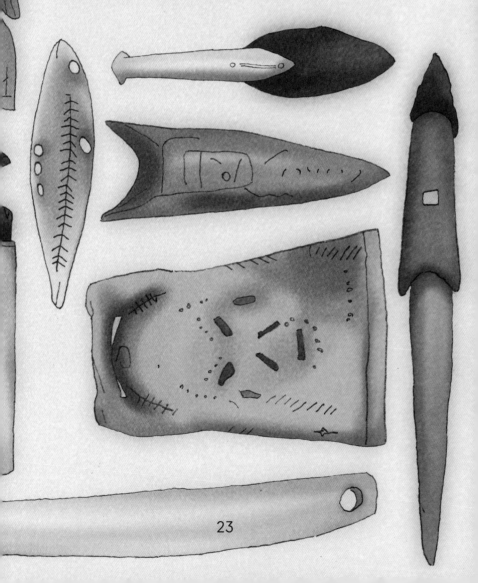

It is said that Tuniit weren't so very different from Inuit in some ways. Tuniit had families, just like Inuit.

Tuniit loved their children and provided for them. We also know Tuniit wore clothing made of animal hides, just like Inuit.

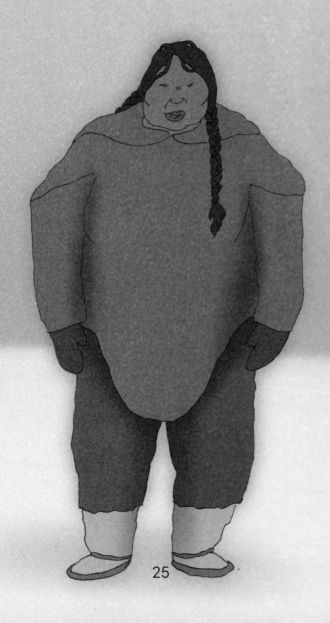

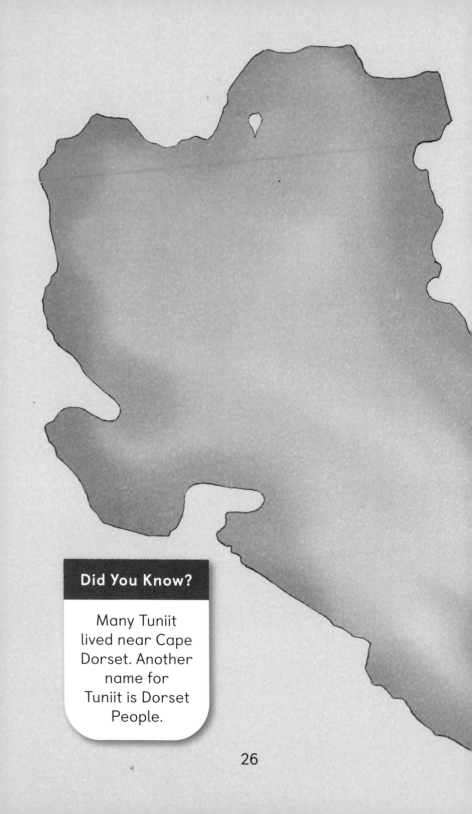

Did You Know?

Many Tuniit lived near Cape Dorset. Another name for Tuniit is Dorset People.

Inuit learned how to live through cold Arctic winters from Tuniit. Inuit tell stories of how their ancestors learned about the best fishing and hunting sites from Tuniit.

It is said that Tuniit taught Inuit how to make inukshuks. Inukshuks are piles of stones that sometimes look like people.

Caribou would see inukshuks and go in the opposite direction, where hunters would wait to catch them.

Did You Know?

Inukshuks are all over Nunavut. One even appears on the flag of Nunavut.

What happened to Tuniit? Some say
a disease killed Tuniit. Some suggest
Inuit took over the best hunting grounds
and Tuniit couldn't survive. Others
say Tuniit and Inuit married and had
children after all, so Tuniit became
part of Inuit.

People have wondered for centuries what happened to Tuniit. Where did these strong, fast hunters go? No matter what, Tuniit live on through the stories told by Inuit.